My Trauma Is My Testimony

Berlesha Palr

REJOICE
Essential Publishing

Berlesha Palmer/Rejoice Essential Publishing
PO BOX 512
Effingham, SC 29541
www.republishing.org

Unless otherwise indicated, scripture is taken from the King James Version.

My Trauma Is My Testimony/Berlesha Palmer

ISBN-13: 979-8-2954-2929-3

Dedication

This book is dedicated to every person who played a role and continues to play a role in my healing process. We know that healing is an ongoing process. Healing never ends. We just get better in time using our tools and resources.

Thank you for being a part of my healing journey.

To my Lord and Savior Jesus Christ, thank you for keeping, saving, and helping me tap into my true given identity of the person you created Berlesha Palmer to be. You get all the glory. Thank you for never leaving me or giving up on me. Your love never fails.

Table Of Contents

ACKNOWLEDGEMENT....vii

INTRODUCTION....1

CHAPTER 1: Disappointments....3

CHAPTER 2: Self-Work -Identify Disappointment....10

CHAPTER 3: Prayer For Releasing And Healing Disappointment....13

CHAPTER 4: My Childhood....14

CHAPTER 5: Prayer For Our Childhood....19

CHAPTER 6: Teenage Years....20

CHAPTER 7: Pray For My Younger Self....24

CHAPTER 8: Teenage Years Being A Mom....25

CHAPTER 9: Adulthood....29

CHAPTER 10: Horrors Of Budget-The Broke Mentality....33

CHAPTER 11: Prayer For Budget And Financial Release....35

CHAPTER 12: The Journal Process –Releasing My Thoughts....36

CHAPTER 13: The Journal Process Prayer....46

CHAPTER 14: Life After Being Broken....47

CHAPTER 15: Life After Being Broken Prayer....51

CHAPTER 16: Life Experiences....52

CHAPTER 17: Life Experiences Prayer....55

CHAPTER 18: Life Connections....56

CHAPTER 19: The Storm....59

CHAPTER 20: The Storm Prayer....65

TABLE OF CONTENTS

CHAPTER 21:	The Loss........66
CHAPTER 22:	The Loss Prayer........67
CHAPTER 23:	Toxic Love........68
CHAPTER 24:	Toxic Love Prayer........70
CHAPTER 25:	Healthy Love........71
CHAPTER 26:	Healthy Love Prayer........74
CHAPTER 27:	Healing........75
CHAPTER 28:	Healing Prayer........80
CHAPTER 29:	Loving You........81
CHAPTER 30:	Loving You Prayer........85
CHAPTER 31:	Spiritual Journey........86
CHAPTER 32:	Spiritual Journey Prayer........89
CHAPTER 33:	Identify Trauma Or Unfortunate Events........90
CHAPTER 34:	Identify Trauma Or Unfortunate Events Prayer........95
CHAPTER 35:	Surround Yourself With A Network Of Support........96
CHAPTER 36:	Seeking Professional Assistance........101
CHAPTER 37:	Seeking Professional Assistance Prayer........104
CHAPTER 38:	Release The Trauma. Working On Your Identity........105
CHAPTER 39:	Release The Trauma. Working On Your Identity Prayer........108
CHAPTER 40:	Show Up And Show Out For You First........109
CHAPTER 41:	Make Peace With Your Past And Give It To God........111
CHAPTER 42:	New beginnings........115
CHAPTER 43:	The Power Of Your Story........118
CHAPTER 44:	What's Next: What Tools Do You Need To Be Successful?........119
CHAPTER 45:	What's Next: What Tools Do You Need

To Be Successful Prayer......124
CHAPTER 46: Scriptures......125
CONCLUSION......127
ABOUT THE AUTHOR......129

Acknowledgement

First and foremost, I would like to thank God for this journey and for always being with me every step of the way, even when it did not feel like He was there. I want to thank my children, who kept me going and helped me want more out of life and strive to become a better person each day. I love y'all. I want to thank my mom for being who she is to me. I want to thank my aunt for always being my listening ear and sounding board. I want to thank Momma Bee and Sherry Washington, who told me years ago I needed to write a book. I want to thank my church family, *New Foundation Church International,* and our leaders Apostle Sam Wagner and Dr. Rico Wagner. I want to thank my therapist, Kim Gray, Bridge of Hope York PA, Michelle Keadle-Taylor, Sharon Lincoln, family, friends and anyone who was part of my journey, good or bad. I appreciate you.

Thank you for being a part of my life, which is now my story.

Victory is ours.

Until next time....

Introduction

This book is for anyone feeling alone, who never felt seen or heard, who went through life trying to find where they belong, whether due to neglect, rejection, abandonment, sexual abuse, physical abuse, emotional abuse, low self-esteem, parent issues, childhood traumas, men or woman issues, safety or daily life issues. No matter the fear or the heartbreak, my hope is that you can find yourself again and be restored through healing and finding your true self-identity while identifying your self-worth. Stay encouraged and know the season you are facing too shall pass. When no one else sees or hears us, please know that God hears and sees us no matter what we are facing in life. He cares for us and wants the very best for us, and He will never leave us. Keep God first all the time.

All relationships start with God. If you are unsure what that means or how to get there, we will dive into this in more detail as you read more. If you have a relationship with God, my hopes are that you will receive a fresh wind, and a gentle reminder of how strong God really is and remember nothing is impossible with God. The best is yet to come, no matter what you have experienced or what you are facing at this very moment. Prayers change things. Take your cares and cast them over to the Lord. Keep praying. He hears your cries, and He will answer you.

Psalm 116: 1 *"I love the Lord, because he heard my voice. He heard my cry for his help."*

Psalm 116:2 *"Because he turned his ear to me, I will call on him as long as I live."*

CHAPTER 1

Disappointments

Did you ever sit back and ask yourself, "Why am I always disappointed? Why do I give my best to people in my life and do right by people, but it never seems like I receive the same in return?" Now remember, we should not give to receive. It does depend on your heart's posture and your intentions and motives. I am speaking to the ones who always move with pure intentions, always do right by others or naturally give to others without expecting anything in return and always end up empty-handed. Typically, with the bare minimum level of respect and with a broken heart, they are used and abused because they are loving with their hearts on their sleeves.

Did you know that this can be a trauma response? From self-identity, lack of love, abandonment issues, momma and daddy issues, past or previous abuse or past experiences that you haven't forgotten or healed from. Most of the time, people like this are truly looking for someone to give them the love they always wanted and never had and honestly wait for someone to show up for them. Longing for someone to prove them wrong, that someone does love them and will show up for them like they do so freely for others. The truth is love is earned and starts with self-love and how you show up for yourself.

Self-Reflection Questions:

1. What are three words that you would use to describe yourself?

____

____

____

____

____

____

2. What does I love you mean to you?

____

____

____

____

____

____

3. Do you take care of yourself?

____

____

____

____

____

____

4. What are some ways you can take better care of yourself?

____

____

____

____

____

____

Many people do not know where to start and how to love themselves. They seek validation from others, places, or things. To love oneself, you must spend time getting to know the deepest parts of yourself; it is not always pretty. Do not allow others to walk all over you because you want to be chosen, seen, or loved. Make sure you have boundaries. Boundaries are where it all begins. Most of us have never been taught the definition of a boundary or how to incorporate boundaries in our lives.

We were taught to give or take from a place of disappointment. The truth is those who want to love you will show up for you. Keep in mind that those who have not worked on themselves or loved themselves first cannot love you or anyone else. Loving someone takes knowing yourself and healing through heartbreaks, traumas, and life experiences. If not, we will all be broken people trying to love others from a place of hurt and disappointment.

In reality, because of life's disappointments, we're breaking others and destroying their lives during our own personal journey and the process of trying to heal and find ourselves while trying to navigate and live life with deeply rooted disappointments. Take your time to work on you for yourself and no one else. You come first before your children, parents, husband, friends, boyfriend/ girlfriend, and career.

Repeat after me: *"I come first and I must put myself first."* In Gloria Leonard, my late grandmother's words, "I have to take care of me." Putting yourself first is not selfish. It is a priority. It shows you know who you are without the need or validation of others. No one can love you better than yourself, but do you know how to love you? Did someone teach you how to love you? Or are you out here learning on your own, repeating the same mistakes and entertaining the same people while things are repeating the same patterns and hitting dead ends in every area of life? Do you feel stuck, like why and how I am here again?

No matter where you are in your journey, please know that you are loved by the love of God and His love will never fail. His love is the best love to have. He will always show up for you and never abandon you. If you have not experienced His love, my hope is that after this book, you will consider the everlasting love that God has to offer you and has had for you before your birth. God is the one consistent love that will not waver. It will not change and it is solid. God's love does not disappoint. People will always disappoint you because they understand from their fleshly views and their life experiences. We all have different views. We were raised differently and experience different things that determine how we love, live, and show up in the world.

Hurt people, hurt people. That is deep, right? When one thinks of love, typically they think of perfect love, a fairy tale love, and the love one experiences in their dreams. There is no perfect love. The only perfect love is from Jesus Christ. Now that we have that settled, let us dig deeper into where we are with the disappointments that life has given us without our permission.

Somehow, we just end up in a world surrounding us in heart break, such as life's experiences and circumstances that try to take us out of this world by ways of depression, bad decisions, reacting out of emotion, and repeated patterns. Somehow, we all managed and made it through while reading this book. Pray for better days or be thankful that you made it through in one piece. What was meant to destroy you only made you stronger and now, you have your story and testimony to share.

Have you asked yourself, "Why am I always disappointed? I give so much and receive so little." Disappointments hurt to the core and each disappointment shatters a piece of your heart and soul. After every disappointment, your identity changes. You start to lose who you are and have less to give and say. At times, you may feel numb from all the disappointments that have occurred in your life, affecting how you show up for yourself and others. Showing up from a hurt place is like not showing up at all. Disappointments are rough. They change your way of thinking. They play tricks on your mind, begin setbacks, and repeatedly shatter your heart. Disappointments festered over into every relationship of your life. Disappointments can cause bitterness and many angry emotions or no emotions at all. Disappointment can take you out of this world if you are not strong enough.

The truth is we are often not strong enough and have to rely on God. What happens when you are disappointed? You lose focus and hope. You begin not to care. You lose emotions and feelings. You become heartless and become ready for revenge. You move through life aimlessly hurt, hurting people without even being aware of how hurt you truly are. When you are disappointed, you want everyone to feel the pain that you felt and all the parties involved in that hurt or disappointed you, you want them to hurt at times how they hurt you. Many of us have different levels of disappointment. You have some people that disappointment is all that they know, so they do not expect anything else; from their point of view everything is negative. All that they experience in life has not been fair to them. Life chose them. They did not choose the life. They see and feel no hope; they are merely here to exist.

With disappointments comes easy fixes. An easy fix could be food, drugs, sex, going from relationship to relationship, addicted to success at their job, and keeping oneself busy to not deal with anything. Those who are disappointed or who have navigated through their life look normal. They interact normally, but deep down inside, they are broken into pieces from life experiences, whether they are from the past, present, or future. Many people will eventually deal with their life's disappointment head-on. Some will hide behind disappointment until life forces them to deal with it and others will die holding on to disappointment because they cannot deal with the heaviness and disappointments.

In most cases, they did not have a listening ear, someone to trust, support, or direction. The battle was too much for them to bear. Disappointments happen to every human being on earth. The difference is the severity of disappointment, the tolerance level, support system, resources, and tools. The truth is disappointments ruin childhoods, identity, and relationships. It depletes who we are by taking our dreams and goals away. In return, it causes a sick, bruised, and wounded heart with no feelings. Disappointment seems like the enemy when it happens, but later, you will see that every disappointment serves a purpose.

Remember, it will take your commitment, dedication, and hard work. Everyone's journey is different. For every disappointment, there is a process of healing. My hope is as you continue to read, you will identify your current disappointments, the ones you may have buried deep down inside and those who disappointed you in hopes of healing and being set free from the bondage that has held you back from your true identity, happiness, greatness, and from living a purposeful life. The truth is we all deserve to be happy and experience the fullness of all life has to offer us. Today is the last day that we will allow our disappointments to hold us hostage and keep us in places where we no longer belong. Today is the day that we begin to identify and heal from our life's disappointments so we can begin to live life and experience all the good things that life has to offer us. Today is the day we begin the work to establish our true self-identity and live as the person God created us to be.

CHAPTER 2

Self-Work-Identify Disappointment.

I, Berlesha Palmer, have been disappointed as a child, not having my father and mother at times. I was disappointed about not having a family like the other kids and families around me. I was disappointed that my grandparents had to take care of me at times when my parents were gone. I was disappointed that I was molested at a very young age and violated. I was disappointed that, at that time, I felt God did not hear or save me. I was disappointed that I begin to search for the meaning of love through sex at a very young age, which resulted in me becoming a teenage mother at the age of 15. I was disappointed being in high school where pregnancy was not normal, and I had to fight for an education. I was disappointed that I was in 10th grade rolling my bookbag from class to class and watching every teacher and student judging me. I was disappointed in myself. How did I become pregnant as a little girl myself?

Learning how to grow up initially this disappointment made me lose hope. I was disappointed my father wasn't there because he made a choice that took him away my entire childhood. During my teenage years and most of my adulthood, he wasn't there to protect me and show me a father-daughter love. I spent my whole life searching for what the meaning of true love and the feeling of love was through temporary fixes. I began to become numb to disappointments. They became normal. It hurt so bad but then they numbed my soul. Now that I am transparent with you and told you a little about my story, it is your turn. It is time to dig in.

Self- Reflection Questions:

1. Make a list of your life's disappointments.

____

____

____

____

____

____

2. Who disappointed you?

____

____

____

____

____

____

3. How has this affected your life?

____

____

____

____

____

____

CHAPTER 3

Prayer For Releasing And Healing Disappointment

Repeat after me: Dear God, where are you? Where were you? I need you now. Reveal all my life's disappointments: the ones I remember clearly and those buried because of pain. Reveal who disappointed me. Reveal the reason and help me identify what this has done to my life. Set me free from all my heartbreaks, from all the people who continue to hurt me and those who I allowed to repeatedly hurt me because I did not know any better or know how to use my voice. Please help me use my resources to bring all the disappointments to life, so that I can deal with each disappointment accordingly and begin my healing process. God, I know you are here with me, and I am never alone, even when no one was there or when I question why you would let bad things happen to me. I release my disappointments, and I give them to you. I know one day, all my disappointments will serve a purpose for your will. I declare healing for my life. I declare vision for my life. I declare for every disappointment a blessing is on the way. The Lord saves and sets me free. Lord, send the support that I need and prepare me for this healing journey. No matter what it looks like, help me build a relationship and to solely rely on you as my source in Jesus's name, Amen.

CHAPTER 4

My Childhood

Our identities start when we are children based on life experiences. I was born in York, Pennsylvania, at York Hospital on July 21, 1986. I lived on what we considered the east-end side of town. From what I can remember, my childhood experiences started at 883 E Kings Court, York, PA, 17403. As a kid, I was surrounded by people but very lonely. I battle with many feelings, such as abandonment and molestation issues. I had to grow up more quickly than most children. When I think of being a kid, they should not have any worries. They should freely play, eat, spend time with family, and enjoy life worry free. I figured out at an early age that it is not always a reality. I was the big sister, so I naturally led, not because I wanted to but because life experiences had placed me in this position.

My father went to prison at a very young age which left me without a father and a split family on my father's side. He was a registered sex offender. For many years, my family kept the secret from me. I am sure to protect me. My grandmother Gloria always kept it real and when the time was right and I was old enough, she told me because she did not want me to find out on the streets. I never told her, but she was too late. Someone else brought it to my attention.

I have always wanted to know why during my childhood, I spent time getting to know my father on the weekends. It involved long car rides, going through metal detectors, and getting quarters to put in the vending machine surrounded by prison guards. I can remember being a kid and happy to see my father, but it felt weird going through metal detectors, seeing guards everywhere and all these men dressed the same with shiny shoes. In my dad's words, I was there, and I knew him. In my words, at what cost was it a traumatic experience? It was not normal; My family did the right thing. They did what was best at that time.

So, my life started off without my father's presence. My mom was around but not consistently every day. My grandmother and great grandmother took care of me and my siblings and did the best that they could. Still, life was not normal like every other family I saw: moms and dads bringing their kids to school, helping them with homework, or having difficult conversations. I was just kind of there trying to figure out if my parents loved me. Of course, they did but growing up, it was hard to explain and convince myself that they did due to the circumstances. There was a lot of history and traumatic experiences tied to that name during my childhood years. Some things I know, and other things I do not. Some things will never be told. Not knowing why, I was not close to my dad's family. It never made sense until I grew older and understood the history.

There was a group of family members who always included me and always made me feel welcome despite the life events that happened. My mother, my best friend during my childhood, was away for most of the time. One day, she decided to try motherhood and give it a chance around my high school year in ninth grade. She worked hard to make it right when she came back into our lives. She maintained our relationship and never gave up on us. She kept a roof over our heads and did her best. She tried to make it right. However, the scars from her absences were in my heart and abandonment was tattooed on my soul. I was a little girl but felt like a little lady holding many things children should not have to think about during childhood.

I was molested by a close friend of my uncles in the house that I grew up in. I learned the word violation during that moment. I realized that people watch everything and evil people will use that to their advantage. I had no parents. My grandparents were older and clueless and were in the house at the time while I was being molested. No one was there to protect me. This is when I became sad because my parents weren't present and I was being violated repeatedly on different occasions, which made me mute to words. At that point, I was there but not mentally present. I remember sitting in school wondering how many other children were being touched, abused, and left behind. How about you? Do you know anyone who was abused or mistreated? Where were you abused as a child? Did you have your parents? What do you remember from your childhood?

Self- Reflection Questions:

Let us reflect on your childhood.

1. What do you remember from your childhood?

____

____

____

____

____

____

2. Do you have good memories from your childhood?

3. Do you have bad memories from your childhood?

4. Did anything happen to you that no one knows?

5. List anything from your childhood that you feel should be released to heal.

____

____

____

____

____

____

CHAPTER 5

Prayer For Our Childhood

Dear God, Lord, help me reveal what to release from my childhood. Help me identify who I need to talk to about my childhood and expose what needs to be done for me to release my childhood experiences to set me free into your destiny and become the person you called me to be. God, release this heaviness, release the disappointment, release the short comings, and help me forgive those who impacted my life traumatically. I know this is the first step to healing. Lord, give me strength as I go back down memory lane. Help me face the harsh realities of the things I have endured or I am enduring now. I have so many questions about my childhood and life experiences and all that comes to me is, "Why me? Why did you let this happen to me and not protect me?" Make it clear. Make it plain. What is your purpose for my life? What blessings will the pain bring to my life? My childhood is heavy, and I no longer want to carry all my childhood experiences in my heart, mind, or words of communication. Bring this to light so I can release it and start to define my true identity and not by my experiences as a child. Lord, I know this may be painful. I ask that you give me the strength and send me the support and resources to get through this. Set me free in Jesus's name. I know you have more for me.

CHAPTER 6

Teenage Years

Whew! Based on what you read, my teenage years were off the chain, as they would say. My period came when I was 12 years old, and I lived with my uncle and his girlfriend, Toya. They spoiled me. I had one of the best Christmases I ever had when I lived with them. I spent most of my teenage years looking for love, trying to figure out what love is supposed to look and feel like. In my teenage years, I was dating and had lots of sex because it felt good at the moment. I thought I was in love a few times, but did not know what love was from a daddy-daughter or a man-woman's perspective. I did not know how to treat and love myself.

Saving yourself until marriage, what did that mean? I was violated since first grade. In my eyes, I was damaged goods already, so why not live my best life and continue to let men use and abuse me? This was very deep. Why not live life feeling good and feeling love through sexual acts, one of the only times I felt seen or heard or loved? This was a lie from the enemy and a trauma response, and I didn't know any better at that time. I planned to have my virginity taken. My virginity was taken by one of the coolest guys in school. We sent letters back and forth and we planned for him to take my virginity like a business meeting. It's crazy but true. He was a player back then and got joy out of hurting girls. Hoping around was his trauma or enjoyment. The truth is we were both two lost kids with fathers in jail and had no guidance, doing what we wanted. By trying to figure it out and navigating through life, we wanted to feel good, be cool, and do what teenagers do by seeking the attention we both lacked. The physical touch felt good, and in the moment, you felt wanted, but that was another lie of the enemy.

The truth is your body is your temple. Do not share it with anyone. Wait until you are married. Do not be used or abused for your body parts. So, I lost my virginity to a man who never was my boyfriend. He never had feelings for me. It was more for the point of the act and the temporary attention. Keep in mind at this point that all I wanted was the attention of a man, someone to love and see me. Once I had sex, I felt like it was love because it felt good, and I had the man's undivided attention. I was on top of the world and then after the act, the void that I always had never went away. My mind still went back to the original questions I had. What is love and what does it feel like? Why does no one choose me?

So, in middle school, having sex felt great and was the prime of my life. The truth is that I was a broken little girl who wanted and needed the love of her parents consistently. I was trying to figure out the huge void in my heart and what was missing, which was so much. Let us start with knowing my worth. At this point, my worth had not been identified. I continued to be heartless, enjoying the moments that took the pain away, but the truth was I was a lost and lonely girl. I let people use and abuse me. They disposed of me when they were done and took advantage of me. That is what I knew. After being hurt repeatedly and played out, this should have been the time that I should have enjoyed my high school years and prepared for the next season of college. I do not share my story because I am proud of it. I share in hopes of saving someone else from being used and abused or to send clarity on what love truly is and what it means to protect their most valuable asset, which is themselves.

Forgive yourself. You did the best that you could with what you had. All your actions were based on the childhood traumas that attracted you to lies and temporary fixes, which, at the moment, felt great. Now, it's your turn.

Self- Reflection Questions:

1. Reflect on your younger self. What were you searching for?

____

____

____

____

____

____

2. What voids were you trying to fill?

____

____

____

____

____

____

3. What advice would you give your younger self?

____

____

CHAPTER 7

Pray For My Younger Self:

Dear God, Thank you for my journey, even if it doesn't make sense now. Everything serves its purpose. Help me release my younger self and my identity at that time. I didn't know any better and all I wanted was love, time, and attention. Forgive me for my sins. Bring up the part that I played in my younger years and revealed. Help me forgive myself for not knowing my worth.

CHAPTER 8

Teenage Years Being A Mom

Teenage years, what was that? I spent my teenage years being a teenage mother. While other teenagers I know were enjoying life and going to the movies and events, I was waking up, changing diapers, making bottles, and building a relationship with my son — a child raising a child. I am thankful for my support system. I was in labor at the age of sixteen. Can you imagine? My body wasn't even develop yet and I was in labor, which is the scariest thing in the world. Having a baby, I knew babies were a gift from God, but I was confused about why and how I got pregnant so young. When my son was born, and I held him for the first time, I remember saying, "Happy Birthday." That was the scariest day of my life and the most life-changing moment.

I value taking care of my child and never letting him down. Everything I did from that moment forward was for him: all the work, tears, and sacrifices. We grew up together. I never had my parents together in one household as a family. So, I also valued never letting my child grow up without me and his dad together. I did not know at the time that it was going to come with a lot of sacrifices. My son witnessed some of the physical, mental, and emotional abuse, embarrassment, and horrible moments. He will never hear or know about some of what I endured. To my younger self, you took a lot more than what you needed to, all for the sake of love. Was it worth it? Maybe not, but this is my story and journey, which has formed me into the woman I am today.

In just a short period, I had so many disappointments. I was missing my mom for some part of my life. I was missing my father for all my childhood and teenage life. I did not have a stable man in my life. Being a teenager, I thought I was old enough to have sex to feel seen and heard, which resulted in me rolling a backpack on wheels through high school while pregnant, fighting for an education. At the time, I was thankful to have a few teachers who cared and wanted to see me succeed. They volunteer to come to my home and homeschool me. One of the teachers told me not to give up because Central High School was responsible for my education and not to let them treat me differently to get my education. I will never forget that the assistant superintendent said, "Well, this is not the typical situation. Teenagers are not getting pregnant."

I did everything to reach out to the NAACP and every resource possible until I received support and help. It was my life, and I was not letting my son grow up without his mother trying to succeed in life. I had to make sure he had a decent life. I felt unstoppable. I was not taking no for an answer. My son changed my life. I honestly feel like my son saved me and my life. The most beautiful blessing in the world was to become a mother. Yes, the timing was not right. My situation was not ideal, but he was a blessing and born into love. No matter what it looked like, my goal has always been never to let him down. None of us are perfect. Sometimes, we intentionally let ourselves down and the people we love most. So, I just did my best.

Self- Reflection Questions:

1. Tell me about a time your life changed quickly.

____

____

____

____

____

____

2. What was the situation? Did you ever tell anyone?

____

____

____

____

____

____

3. How did you handle it? What did you learn out of the moment? What are you most proud of?

____

____

____

____

4. Does anything from this moment impact your life today?

CHAPTER 9

Adulthood

At this stage of life, I was broken from so many experiences. I just had enough. Has anyone ever asked you, "Who are you?" Can you answer it besides saying a mom or explaining your job or significant other? Someone asked me who I was, and I remember saying, "Wow! Who am I?" I could not answer the question. That insistently made me sad. Who am I? Until I could define who I naturally was, I took each day to teach me, heal, and take a journey down memory lane. I would drive past my old childhood houses and relive some amazing memories and horrible moments. However, it was all part of my healing process. Healing takes time. Believe it or not, it requires taking a hard, deep look at how you see yourself: under the layers, your pretty or ugly face.

We are all beautiful creations of God, but life can show you something different. Your childhood, experiences, and people you were around could affect the way you view yourself. There are many lies we have told ourselves over the years.

- No one loves me.
- No man stays in my life.
- Everyone wants to get over on me.
- Everyone in my life is here to take, take, and take.

- I was made to give, give, and give and receive nothing in return."

Some other lies are:

- I don't deserve better.
- Let me stay because no one else will love me.
- Let me have sex because it feels good and that's when I am seen.
- Let me hide behind my fashion.
- Let me stay busy, so I don't have to deal with myself.
- Let me stay busy, so I do not have to think about painful memories.
- Those memories make me a bad person.
- I will never live past the pain in my life.
- I will not survive and there is no need to live.

The above thoughts are lies from the enemy, so you can stay stuck and not discover what God has for you. It is time to be set free. No one can hold you back from your healing but you. Let us start by taking inventory of our lives. Remember that you must be ready for all the things that may arise. Some things you may remember clearly. Others may have been so hurtful you buried so far in your soul that you forgot about it. As we reflect on the past, remember no one is off limits when inventorying who hurt and who caused us pain. Most people who caused us pain didn't even realize how bad it was. Some intentionally took advantage of us. In some cases, we had no choice but to allow them to take advantage of us, depending on our self-esteem and how comfortable we are saying, "No."

Self- Reflection Questions:

1. Were you raised to be a people pleaser?

____

____

2. Do you only feel noticed when you are around many people?

3. Do you feel safe when there is confusion and lots of noise?

4. Do you feel unsafe when you are alone and things are quiet?

____

____

____

____

Please take a moment to identify how you feel about yourself. Now ask yourself, "Who am I?" If you are stuck, it is time to do some research. Begin to write this down: I am ______________________________. In my case, I wrote, I am Berlesha Palmer. I did not realize it would take years to figure out who I was. I started my healing journey the day I started to find out who Berlesha was. Please note that healing is a journey. It never ends. Some days will be good, bad, or unbearable. I had many nights crying myself to sleep because the memories and healing were painful. All I could do was call out to God and ask Him, "Where are you? Come save me?"

The healing process wore me down. I was sad most days, so I isolated myself. You may think I isolated myself so people could not see me unhappy. However, it was so I could be still and not hear noise or distractions around me. I remember the scripture that kept coming to mind was, "Be still and know that I am God." I thought that was my sign to be still and not make any changes. As I continued to grow, I learned that is not what this scripture meant. Through my healing journey, I learned to trust God and gained a deeper meaning of the scripture.

CHAPTER 10

Horrors of Budget- The Broke Mentality

No one taught me anything about budgeting growing up. All I remember was everyone spending, being messed up, struggling, living paycheck to paycheck. Of course, I knew I did not want to be messed up financially when I got older, but that did not prevent me from spending. I would make money and spend it. I knew it was a bad habit, but it never affected anything and always felt good. I would just be broke until payday. I did not look broke, but I stayed broke. I did not enjoy getting paid bi-weekly. It was always the longest two weeks. I quickly made living paycheck to paycheck my lifestyle. Credit? What is that? I have never heard of it.

One time, in ninth grade, we had a class that taught us about money and saving. By then, I was already over it and it was too much to learn. So, I grew up ready to make money and to save money. Let's not forget that I didn't have many happy moments. So, I grew up wanting to make beautiful memories at any cost because memories matter to me. I went broke for memories. I was evicted for memories. I risked it all for memories. For most of my life, when it came to money, I was always in survival mode, which meant I was always behind, moving bills around, and still participating in activities I couldn't afford to add another beautiful memory.

Please keep in mind that I had decent jobs and made decent money during this time. The problem was I never knew how to budget. When someone tried to teach me, I just never understood it. I inherited the broke mentality and that was my lifestyle. It did not matter if I was broke. I did not look like it, which was another lie of the enemy. There are principles to budgeting, credit, and saving that will provide a fulfilling life if you follow them. Plan, budget your money and save for rainy days. Do not go broke trying to prove a point to others. Your identity is not based on how much money you have, what you wear, or anything materialistic. It is so much deeper than that. Consistently review your budget weekly or monthly. Hold yourself accountable to your spending habits. Ask yourself: Is this a need or a want? Take a moment to reflect on how you feel when you spend. This is attached to a feeling. Money should not complete or identify you. How and what you spend your money on can also be a trauma response to what you never had. Do not let money hold you hostage to a place you do not belong.

CHAPTER 11

Prayer For Budget And Financial Release

Dear God, please show me what the value of money means to me and what it has caused in my life. Set me free of attaching my worth to material things, to not having in my childhood or going without. Money is not my identity. Materialistic things do not prove who I am. I pray for the true identity of what money means to me and for the release of what money should mean. I pray for a financial increase. No more lack and I receive an abundance of money to live debt-free. I pray that when I receive the blessings, I am financially prepared to be a good financial steward and follow the godly principles of money. I release the broke mentality and all the hindrances that money has used to hold me back from receiving an overflow. I declare and decree that I will have more than enough money to meet my financial needs. Help teach me the importance of budgeting and stewarding my money. Teach me the biblical principles to manage money. Break every soul tie and the lies that I have attached to money that have been holding me back from a breakthrough. In Jesus' name. Amen.

CHAPTER 12

The Journal Process-Releasing My Thoughts.

1. Have you ever had thoughts and feelings with nowhere to put them?

2. Have you ever felt lonely without having much to say?

3. Have you ever felt overwhelmed with no outlet?

4. Have you ever felt like you did not have anyone to trust or listen to you?

5. Have you ever felt like people you confided in would listen but not understand?

6. What do you do with those feelings? Hold them in? Do you let them tear you up on the inside while trying to maintain your composure?

7. Have you ever found yourself in the middle of a storm with no one to turn to or talk to without judging you?

8. What do you do when you find yourself in this situation?

____

____

____

____

Try to write down all your feelings. Express your feelings and get them out of your system. In 2018, my life fell apart. Anything that could have gone wrong did. I tried to do everything to pull myself together and look normal to everyone else. My children cannot see me fall and struggle. I had to keep going and fighting even if I did not want to because they needed me. I was so weak and ready to give up.

When I was younger, I went to church, but I realize now that God heard, saw, and was always watching over me. Yet, in the middle of losing and fighting for everything, I began to journal my thoughts and feelings. As I began to journal, I realized that it helped me release all my feelings and it would never go as far as the pages that I wrote it on because it was between me, the page. and God. The more I journaled my thoughts and feelings, the more I realized how important it is to talk about and release my feelings and emotions.

I never remember journaling as a child. It was almost like my mind was the journal. When I moved from Florida back to Pennsylvania as an adult, my life had completely fallen apart. I was lower than I ever had been in life. I was not perfect, but I tried to keep myself together. I maintained a house, a car, and the basic things you need to be a mother until I lost everything. Can you imagine losing everything and then one day seeing the purpose of the loss? In those moments, I did not realize I was in so much pain and how broken I really was. Being broken started as a child when my parents left me for reasons of their own. Even though I was always surrounded by love, all I really wanted was for my parents to choose me first. A void of abandonment was formed and I carried it because of their absence.

Now that I am older, I realize they did their best. I realize that they were parents only at their level of understanding. However, as a child, I always wondered what could be more important than being with your children. I also grieved losing my boyfriend. According to him, he was the best boyfriend I ever had. He was the right one, but we were together at the wrong time. I truly believe timing is everything. If anything, he taught me how a real man should always treat me. I left him not because I wanted to but because of the circumstances of our relationship. I was losing myself and I had to choose me. He supported me, but it hurt both of us. I always wished him well because he deserves happiness and so do I.

Healing began in the season when my life was falling apart. Without the trials and tribulations, I would not know who I am and my worth today. The trials and tribulations made me look at myself. It made me realize how hurt I have been for years, from deaths in my family to being cheated on, mistreated in my earlier relationships of life, and being abused physically, mentally, and emotionally. I have been manipulated my whole life in some ways because of my caring, loving heart and the need to be chosen and loved. I strongly believe what you give out into this world comes back to you. I am not perfect but I have always tried to treat people the way I want to be treated. There are two famous sayings, "What goes around, comes around," and "Karma is real."

When I came back home, I had already tried to move two other times. First, to North Carolina. Then, to Florida. Let's talk about my move to North Carolina. The second time I went back to North Carolina, I got pregnant and was scared. I received my degree, which was positive, while in North Carolina. Afterward, I moved to Florida while grieving my grandmother's death. Not knowing at the time, you take you with you wherever you go. You can't run from yourself. All the hurt, pain, or disappointments follow you to any state, home, or relationship. That is a hard pill to swallow when you are not ready to deal with yourself. Life teaches you that, at some point, you must deal with yourself. Here I was with all the broken pieces shattering. My heart, every person I cared for and loved, was gone. I was left with myself, looking in the mirror, asking myself, "What happened to you? What happened to me, Berlesha Palmer and how did we get here?" I was just broken into pieces, wandering around in my head, laying lifeless, and heartbroken, not knowing how to fix it and most importantly, I was lost and disappointed. How did I get here not knowing who I was or what to do? This did not make sense to me.

The hurt, disappointments, and life experiences changed me. Who am I? At that moment, I could not answer that question. What does she like to do? Who is she without using her kids and job to describe her? I realized over the years I lost myself and my identity. I had to figure out who I was. I knew I had to dig deep and go back to the people and experiences that made me lose my identity:

- the seven year old little girl
- the teenager looking for love
- the teenage mother fighting her way past the judgement
- the woman who was the people pleaser. She pleased people who took advantage of her.
- the mother
- and the broken me.

This was the day I knew I had to start working on myself and journaling in partnership while talking to a professional who did not know my story, but they could help me without judging me. This is where my journal process began.

Self- Reflection Questions:

1. Who are you? Please remember not to use "I am a mother or a father," or your job or profession.

____

____

____

____

____

____

2. Who are you without those things? Can you answer this question?

____

____

____

____

____

____

If not, this is where the road to your self-identity will begin. Start with my name is ____ and I am ____ ____. Begin to write and keep in mind this may take some time. You may feel stuck, but keep going. Be patient with yourself and give yourself grace. It may take hours, days, or years.

If you are like me, it took years and even now, I still have journals from 2018. I journaled about my life, the ups, downs, struggles, goals, hopes, and dreams. I learned, grew, and prayed a lot. I overcame so much. You can do this too. Today is the day you start to explain who you truly are. I went to Ross to purchase journals for $2.99. The journals had scriptures inside that always seemed to align with my season of life. I found out a lot about myself by spending time alone and journaling.

Self- Reflection Questions:

1. After you write, tell me who you are.

____

____

____

____

____

____

2. What lessons have you learned over the years?

____

____

____

____

____

____

3. Do you have repeated patterns? Can you pinpoint where they stem from?

4. Was digging deep easier for you? Are you real with yourself and where are you now?

5. Do you need help and are there painful experiences you do not want to admit to?

6. What do you need to help your journal out? Do you like this? Did journaling help you? Why or why not?

CHAPTER 13

The Journal Process Prayer

Dear Lord, we are thankful for you. For those who may not know you or have experienced your goodness, reveal your purpose for their lives. Also, for those who have had bad experiences and questioned why they were going through a tough time, please reveal your purpose for their lives. Please show them you are always there through the good, bad, and ugly times. Open their minds and hearts. Help them release all the secrets, pain, and disappointment to you through journaling so they can leave it there. Lord, provide the next steps and help us heal so we can begin to reach out to the people and resources to receive peace and understanding. Most importantly, help them find purpose in their true identities. In Jesus' name, Amen.

CHAPTER 14

Life After Being Broken

When you are not ready or too tired to fight, most of the time, life will break you down. Most of us have been fighting all our lives. Healing is a lifetime journey. It's hard and painful. There are ups and downs. One day, you will be sad. On another day, you will be happy. Some days, you feel like you're winning; on others, you will feel like life has fallen apart. It is all part of the process. Remember, everyone's healing journey will look different. People must do what works for them. Our journey is ours. It is not for anyone else to understand. We must follow our process and learn what is right and wrong for us. There are no right or wrong answers. The moment I realized this, I became free and started to heal from life after being broken, after so many losses. I knew I did not want to keep living hurt, depleted, tired, and miserable. I knew I wanted the happy Lesha back, who was the go-getter Lesha back.

Since 2018, I have been determined to heal and find myself again. So, life outside of being broken started to feel good. It all started with me knowing who I was and what I deserved. It was a maintenance situation. I continued to teach and ask myself many questions. Who are you? What do you like to do? What adds to your happiness? Anything making you happy is a lie. People, places, and things can only add to your happiness. You must be happy with yourself. You must be happy within before anything else can add to your happiness. It all starts with you. I remember asking myself, "Can I make myself happy?"

Well, let's start by learning what I like to do. I enjoy traveling, lying on the beach, and reading encouraging books to pour into my spirit. I have always been adventurous, but I started taking more adventures by meeting new people and trying new things. I took myself outside of my comfort zone and learned who I was. I took my time and did not allow outside people to interfere with my inner work and inner healing that had to take place. There is a life outside of being broken. The truth is, I will always have broken pieces that I am discovering while working to find myself and become more connected with my true, authentic self. I am the person who God created. The lies of the world, people's opinions, or my life experiences did not create me. Life after being broken takes lots of prayers, journaling, encouragement, support groups, step backs, evaluation, soul searching, and switching things up.

Life after a breakdown feels great. I am no longer operating as a victim or from a place of abandonment. I am no longer operating from neglect or a person in lack. I am operating more as my authentic self. I am more whole, loved, healed, and satisfied with the woman that I am becoming. I am at peace knowing that every day will not be perfect. Every day will bring something new. I will still hurt and have pain. Being human and feeling the pain, hurt, and disappointment is okay. Journal and release your thoughts and feelings if you do not want to tell anyone because of fear of being judged. Keep working on yourself, no matter what it looks like. Remember, your story will not look like anyone else. Do what makes you happy and keep working on yourself for you. Never give up on yourself and your happily ever after, no matter how crazy things seem.

Self- Reflection Questions:

1. After the broken years of your life, what added to your happiness?

2. How did you find yourself again? What held you back?

3. What does a good day look like? What does a bad day look like?

4. What were the obstacles sent to destroy you?

5. How did you overcome the obstacles sent to destroy you?

CHAPTER 15

Life After Being Broken Prayer

Lord, we thank you for giving us the strength never to give up. As we move forward in life, we ask that you continue showing us your love and power in directing our steps to what is next. We ask that you expose the unhealed wounds in our bodies so we can heal, nurture, release, and bind them up in Jesus' name. Set us free from the bondage of our past. Give us discernment to see what is holding us back. Lord, if we don't know who you are and what you are capable of doing, please make it clear to us and pull us closer to you for healing and to set our souls free from setbacks and bondage that's holding us hostage in becoming the best healed version of ourselves. Thank you, in Jesus' name, Amen.

CHAPTER 16

Life Experiences

We all have life experiences we could have gone without. We all have life experiences that we need to learn lessons to make us stronger, to hit rock bottom, and to excel to the top. Without God, we are nothing. He directs our paths, the people in the path, and the situations that come to destroy, break, and hinder us. All are part of our journey. Have you ever asked yourself why? Why was I given this life to survive? Listen, I asked myself all the time. Lord, why me and when will it change? There were times in my life I asked God, "Why me and why did you choose me to struggle so much? I am tired of so many losses and working so hard and not seeing them pay off. I am tired of the struggle. God, where are you? I cannot take another day."

I never really viewed life experiences as preparing us for something greater and bigger than we see. I never viewed life experiences as the purpose for our lives to help others. I never viewed life experiences created to make us stronger. I viewed my life experiences as unfortunate. I experienced my life experiences as me getting the bad end of the stick. My life experiences were painful, but there's nothing a little prayer, journaling, and therapy could not fix.

Self- Reflection Questions:

1. What life experiences hurt you?

2. What life experiences made you stronger?

3. What life experiences have you had to turn the pain into purpose?

4. What life experiences are you still holding on to?

5. What life experiences have unanswered questions? Who has the answers?

CHAPTER 17

Life Experiences Prayer

Lord, reveal to me all the life experiences that I buried and wanted to forget. Bring to the surface the life experiences that may be holding me back. Lord give me the strength to acknowledge what happened and what work needs to be done to heal from those experiences that took away my happiness, mind, feelings, and happy attitude. I want the loving, happy, outgoing, and healthy version of myself back. Lord, direct my steps. Give me the discernment to learn who's healthy for me and who is not. Keep revealing who is in my support system and corner and those who are here to distract. Lord, release me from the strong holds of my life experiences. I am working to be free. Lord, free me from everything holding me back and not aligned with your purpose for my life in Jesus' name, Amen.

CHAPTER 18

Life Connections

You will connect with people who drain, uplift, and encourage you in life. People will tear you down. People will show you their true colors if you don't do things the way they want. People will speak to your traumas and hurt places that will keep you stuck. Healthy connections are important. There will be a time when you will meet someone in passing, who will give you a message you will never forget that will linger with you in your soul, a voice you will always hear and remember. In my case, all my managers poured, uplifted, and encouraged me throughout my career. They looked out for me.

I was in partnership with Bridge of Hope, where Michelle and my neighbor volunteer group, Deb, Debbie, Joanne, Allison, Tracy, and Stacey, changed my life forever. They either gave me an encouraging word, prayer, a ride, money, cooking me dinner, or took me out to dinner. I looked up to the role models that God has placed in my life. No matter what, He leads, guides, protects, and brings me a step closer to trusting people again. Miss Sharon walked me through repentance and all of the life choices that I made from being scared of pain. She brought to my attention the root cause of the hurt that I did not want to let go of. She believed and encouraged me to get better. My grandmother was my rock and everything. I am grateful for everything she did because she never missed a beat in my life. I am forever thankful for my grandparents, parents, sister, brother, and uncle. Since I was a little girl, my aunt poured every chance she had into me. She was my listening ear for everything, including my failures and accomplishments.

Ellen from Boscov always took up for me and gave me an opportunity in the retail world while I was a teenage mother in high school. Miss Mary Wilt-Smith believed in me and helped me start my banking career. Christie Winters and Kristen Ferree motivated and taught me everything they knew. Miss Karen, who I consider my partner, also taught me everything she knew. For so many years, she wanted to see me win and provided support, an ear and encouragement.

I am truly thankful for Michelle because she helped me learn and heal. She taught me how to be a better mother, love God again, and forgive Him. She reminded me that I came from a praying family that prays. As a result, I could trust, love again, and be vulnerable again. Her teaching revealed patterns that were holding me back from greatness.

Erin was another divine connection in my life because she was flexible, gave me a chance, and offered rides when I did not have a car. She went above and beyond any manager's expectations. I'm grateful for Della because she listened to the Holy Spirit and gave me a chance. She helped me identify what I enjoy doing most in my HR career. She was a leader and committed warrior of God.

I'm thankful for Ellen. I call her warrior, fighter, and hero. She made a difference by loving, rooting for, and provided opportunities for everyone in the workplace. Elgin is another divine connection. He is my listener because his spirit was always so calm. I consider him a true leader, who led by example. He was always there and taught me so much with grace and honor. Dennis thank you for being apart of my journey and making an impact throughout the different seasons of my life.

Maya taught me patience, the power of not reacting, the power of planting seeds, and the power of overcoming and enjoying God's work. She also taught me the power of hanging in there even when you want to give up, the power of the poker face, and the power of listening before responding. I received daily reminders before my workday started of being who I was called to be. I learned many lessons from each person I listed above and I can never say thank you enough. I wish each of them blessings beyond their sight. I thank God for their faithfulness and dedication to my life. I am grateful for them being faithful to God's work they have done in my life.

Lawrence was the friend I didn't know I needed. I am thankful for his wisdom and encouraging words. I appreciate him loving and accepting me for who I am, my flaws and all. We had many years of arguments, yet he provided a listening ear. Most importantly, Lawrence helped me back to the path of finding Berlesha again, without even knowing it. Our journey was a beautiful one. I am forever thankful because he is an inspiration not only to me but to so many others. I am thankful for my unit that helped me survive in any way, shape, or form. The Grant family, Palmer Family, and all my friends, exes, and family all played a part in my journey, and I love them all.

CHAPTER 19

The Storm

The definition of a storm is a violent disturbance of the atmosphere, moving angrily or forcefully in a specified direction, suddenly attacked and captured using force. Have you ever been hit from the left out of nowhere by something devasting that you did not see coming? Have you experienced hurt or pain from those you loved or thought were in your corner? It could have been family, friends, loved ones, your spouse, children, associates, or connections. Just remember, as we go through this portion of the journey, there is no victory without a storm. The storm is there to grow you. In the moment of the storm, it seems as if things are impossible. It seems like things are falling apart.

In my storm, I lost my job making, the most money I ever had. It was a blessing when I took the job and I felt like this had to be God. He opened this door for me and my family. Then, one day, I experienced something unexplainable, but I knew this was not what God had for me. I spent months trying to get a job. No one was calling me, which was odd because someone was always calling me. When I was looking for a job, it was silent. I heard nothing and no one was calling. There were sounds of crickets. I used my savings to keep my household stable, but the savings were running low. Bills were piling up, but I kept praying. I was denied unemployment at first. It was a whirl wind. My life was in shambles.

I was trying to hold it together and pray my way through it. In the middle of that storm, another one came that almost took me out. Someone called the police on my uncle, who was facing stage three cancer, for an old warrant. I cried and wept because I knew he was going to die in jail. Unfortunately, the jail system does not care about those who are terminally ill. The person who called the police knows who they are. I forgave them because God gave me the victory. My heart was broken. How could anyone be so evil to want to see someone die and rot in jail? Jealousy is deadly.

In my 38 years of life, this was the first time that I was so broken that I felt like I would never be the same. I was devasted, lonely, afraid, angry, depressed, and sad. One morning, my daughter and I walked outside, and the car was gone. Thankfully, I was always transparent with my children, and they were aware of the situation. At this point, I was so tired of fighting; I just nicely said the car was gone. I knew exactly what happened and who caused it, but I knew my God would never let me lack a thing and He did not. What the enemy meant for evil, God meant for good.

I was abused when I thought I was in love. I will never forget never realizing that the man I was with did not love me. He cheated on me with multiple women. He impregnated two other women at the same time as me. One day, he hit and bruised me. I remember touching my face and thinking, "You wanted a family so badly because you didn't have your mom and dad growing up. You are letting a man hurt you and your kids are watching." The last time my face was bruised, I will never forget rubbing my face and looking in the mirror asking, "How did you get here? It is never too late to get out." I did and when I did, I never looked back. It took a lot of tears, heartache, and pain to gain the courage to get out.

I was abused as a young girl. I became a teenage mother. I suffered and I struggled my entire life to be the best mom and beat the odds of teenage pregnancy and not graduating from high school. My son was facing jail time. I spent my whole life trying to raise him not to be in the streets, but he grew up and chose his own path, and he was facing a lot of jail time. This is one of the most devasted things that can happen, watching your child in court in front of a judge who can sentence them to years behind bars. My son is a fighter. He wanted to fight it. I know they would make an example out of my son. I prayed and rocked back and forth. I was devastated at this point. I tried to keep it all together, but I was falling apart.

Many of the storms, we cannot put into words. We feel like we are suffocated, and no one is there. I remember crying to God and asking Him every night and day, "Where are you? Lord, I cannot take no more. Do not let another thing happen." I had no strength to want to move forward in life. I had no job. My son was facing jail time. I was paying bills with no help, trying to run a household. Jealousy and evil spirits were being used to tear my family apart. My uncle was diagnosed with cancer and now I saw his mug shot in jail by looking him up online. All I can remember saying is, "Lord, what did I do to deserve this?" which was a lie from the enemy.

The storm is designed to harm, set us back, kill, and destroy us; God will always have the victory. The storm taught me that the enemy will use those closest to you. Sometimes, the ones you love and would do anything for will hurt, harm, and destroy you! The spiritual meaning of a storm can mean renewal and transformation. Always remember the purpose of God's storms is to prove His unfailing love for us and to grow our faith (Psalm 107:28-31). Trust the storms of your life. God will have the victory. Remember, the storm is the test of your faith to help you grow and trust God to fight your battles. Storms involve many feelings, emotions, hills, and valleys, but God will restore. You have the victory.

Repeat after me: I am safe in God's arms. I am protected by God. Nothing and no one can harm me. The Lord will protect me and give me strength and peace through every storm of my life.

Self- Reflection Questions:

1. What storms are you holding on to that has affected your life?

____

____

____

____

____

____

2. What storms do you need to release to be set free?

____

____

____

____

____

____

3. Who do you need to forgive?

4. What storm are you currently facing?

5. Who disappointed you?

6. **What are you feeling at this moment:** sadness, depression, defeat, weakness, unworthiness? List all your feelings here.

____

____

____

____

____

____

7. What do you need at this very moment?

____

____

____

____

____

____

CHAPTER 20

The Storm Prayer:

Dear Lord, we come before you right now, asking you to touch the people reading this book. Lord, you know all the storms they have faced and will encounter in the future. I ask for the release of the memories of the storms, which are overbearing and taking over their minds and hearts. Lord, support them through the storm. I asked you to send the resources and people they need to defeat the storm. Bless them to draw closer, surrender, and cast all their care to you. We ask for supernatural healing of their minds, bodies, and souls. We ask for a new way of thinking as we face the storms of life. We ask for discernment of those surrounding us causing the storms. Thank you, Lord. We rest tonight knowing you are working on our behalf and it is already done because you said so. Refresh us Lord and give us peace that surpasses all understanding. The storm will not last forever and the blessings are on the way in Jesus' name. Lord, set the person who is reading this prayer free. Touch their lives, hearts, souls, and circles in Jesus's name. Amen.

CHAPTER 21

The Loss:

Have you ever lost something for which you were not ready? Have you ever woken up one day and someone you loved was not there? One day, they are just gone. This is the most heart-wrenching pain in the world. The loss of a loved one, someone you care about, someone you see every day or with whom you grew up with, or someone who may not know as much but you know they are family. I feel like to be so young in life, I have had so many losses, too many to name one by one. I learned each time someone left me, I lost a piece of myself. When I was in elementary school, I felt so lucky. I had my grandparents on my mother's side and father's side and my great grandmother. Many other children did not have their grandparents or great grandparents with them. As I grew older, I started to experience the meaning of loss, and it was not until I was about 37 years old that I understood I had to grieve and I did not have to be strong all the time. I learned that if I needed to lay in bed for a few days, journal, surround myself with others for support, therapy sessions, talk to a friend, or just pray, it was okay.

CHAPTER 22

The Loss Prayer

Lord, help us rest in you and your love in the time of grief. Lord, send the resources to help us navigate through life as we lose loved ones. Lord, heal the holes in our hearts that only you heal. Help us to cast all of your care and worries on to you. Help us see that there is a life worth living after losing so much in Jesus' name. Amen.

CHAPTER 23

Toxic Love

Toxic love is something I pray that most people do not have to experience. Whether it is in your younger years, you witnessed toxic love and thought it was the norm, whether someone mistreated you and you never healed, so you mistreated others. No matter how it goes, your heart was broken by your parents, girlfriend, boyfriend, spouse, or a boo thing. Toxic love is trying to be seen, chasing love, trying to force someone to love you, not knowing your worth and settling for mistreatment while being set up to be second and played around like a game of chess. Toxic love is playing with one emotion in their heart and stringing them along. Toxic love is allowing someone to do these things to you.

Toxic love is not seeing your worth and value while settling for anything that is given to you just to be seen or heard. Toxic love is running back to the person who hurt or uses you with no intent of loving you properly. Toxic love is playing repeated games with a man's heart or woman's heart with no intention to love them properly. Toxic love is to stay connected with someone because of a physical attachment that offers nothing in return. Toxic love is dealing with someone for years with no commitment, goals, or growth. Toxic love is having multiple partners because you are unsure what you bring to the table. Toxic love is staying connected to an ex while moving forward with someone else. Toxic love is having no respect for yourself.

Self- Reflection Questions:

1. Who in your life is toxic? Why do you allow them to hold you back?

____

____

____

____

____

____

2. Why do you continue to deal with them?

____

____

____

____

____

____

3. Do you think you do not deserve better?

____

____

____

____

____

____

CHAPTER 24

Toxic Love Prayer:

Lord, we pray that you give us eyes to see and ears to hear. Who in our lives do we need to release? Who in our lives are examples of your love? We release any identity that keeps us attached to toxic love. We ask for provision to identify what is pleasing in your sight, who should be in our lives, and who should be removed. We rely on you Lord to reveal those who are toxic in our lives and holding us in bondage. Give us the strength and wisdom to know when to let go in Jesus' name. Amen.

CHAPTER 25

Healthy Love

Love is patient. Love is kind. It does not envy or boast. Love bears all things, believes all things and endures all things. Love never fails. Love is explained in 1 Corinthians 13:4-8. The love of God is everything you need to overcome and get through any storm. The Lord is consistent and he never gives up on us. He wants the best for us and His love is unconditional. No love is greater than the love of the Lord. Get to know Him and taste and see for yourself. His love never fails. Trust Him and His love and He will direct your paths and guard your heart during every season of your life. Healthy love is knowing who you are in Christ, knowing who you are as a person, and identifying and healing the wounds of your past. It includes cleansing your soul, unlearning all the negative things, and releasing all the setbacks and pain that held you hostage all your life or for a specific season. Healthy love includes forgiveness of your and other's shortcomings. Forgive them for the hurtful and painful impact they caused. Most importantly, forgive yourself for allowing mistreatment of things that you not deserve or things outside of the Lord's will for your life. Healthy love feels safe and secure. Healthy love shows up for you and will never have you guessing where you stand by putting anyone before you.

Self- Reflection Questions:

1. What does healthy love mean to you?

____

____

____

____

____

____

2. Who in your life demonstrates healthy love?

____

____

____

____

____

____

3. What is holding you back from receiving or giving healthy love?

____

____

____

____

4. Do you think you deserve healthy love?

CHAPTER 26

Healthy Love Prayer

Lord, I pray that those reading this book will experience your love and the true definition of unconditional, healthy, and unwavering love. I asked that you reveal what is holding them back from healthy love in Jesus' name. Amen.

CHAPTER 27

Healing

Healing takes time and work. Be patient with yourself. Your healing process will not look like anyone else's. Your journey will feel and look different. Your healing journey is there to make you strong when you are weak. The healing journey will have you face situations with people you may have been avoiding or running from your entire life. If you do not heal from things or people that disappointed, violated, hurt, mistreated, misused, and abused you, they will win while you are held in this victim state of mind. The victim state of mind will hold you captive to all the things from your past. It will hinder you from moving forward.

Healing is necessary to cleanse your body from the inside out. It does not matter how you look on the outside if the inside is bruised, hurt, disappointed, confused, scared, and tired, which will eventually shine through to the outside. Healing and taking care of you means learning about yourself, spending alone time, addressing the issues that are holding you back, and hearing how you feel about what happens to you and what hurts you. For many years, I had to heal from self-love, abandonment, molestation, and physical and mental abuse. Still, I am so proud that I received deliverance during my journey. I overcame a lack of love issues for various reasons:

- I was addicted to success and thought it was my identity.

- I was addicted to men who were not good for me. They used me because I allowed them to manipulate me just for some attention.
- I settled for the bare minimum and wondered why my life stayed at a standstill for so long.
- I overcame being second in careers and relationships.

I often did not believe I deserved good things because all I knew were bad things and struggles. Healing is messy. You must go to places you do not want to go; you must dig deep into the issue at hand to the core. You may have to visit your childhood, where it all begins. The lack begins there. Whether you had no parents or one parent present, your identity starts in childhood. It is when you learn who you are: good, bad, or indifferent.

Our childhood is the foundation of our beliefs. Depending on what your childhood showed or exposed to you, can determine what you believe today. Take time to deal with what has been in your heart and mind that has slowly been eating your soul over decades. The goal is to identify what hurts or disappoints you. Identify and speak it out. Depending on the situation, address it with the parties involved, a doctor, and a therapist. It is okay to ask for help, which is why we have these parties in their professions to help guide, lead, and free us.

Self- Reflection Questions:

1. What do you need healing from? It seems like an easy question, but it may take some time to identify the root cause.

____

____

____

2. Who disappointed you and why?

3. Who hurt you?

4. Who took advantage of you? Do they know what they did? Do other people know?

5. Have they done this to other people? How does it make you feel?

6. Take a moment and close your eyes. Where do you feel pain? What part of your body is the most painful?

7. When do you feel sad? What triggers your sadness?

8. When do you feel angry? What triggers your anger?

Start there. Start slow if needed, but just start. This is not a race. This is your journey. It will be messy and uncomfortable, but you got this, and God has you. This is one of the steps that will set you free from bondage.

CHAPTER 28

Healing Prayer

Lord, heal our hearts and souls by freeing our minds of distraction. Let us focus on you and the pain. Help us identify where the root of the pain is located in our bodies. Reveal to us where the stem and the root have formed so that we can heal our bodies in agreement with your words and guidance. Lord, give us the strength to free ourselves from this hurt. Give us the strength to connect and partner with those in the best interest of our healing. Lord, remind us that you are always there. When we are alone and afraid, let us cry out to you for guidance and direction. We pray for the right help and resources to help us. Lord, give us strength as we want to heal to become better and peaceful people who are not broken. We pray for wholeness and restoration. In Jesus' name, amen.

CHAPTER 29

Loving You

Whew! Loving you. It sounds so easy, but how does love look and feel? Who taught you how to love yourself? Some people do not know what love is, nor do they know how to love themselves. It is hard to love correctly without loving yourself first. I am still on a journey of loving myself. It is not about saying, "I love me." It is also believing I love myself when things get ugly, when I am disappointed or rejected when life shakes up a bit and when I am tired and want to give up. Have you ever wanted to give up? What was the reason and why did that happen? I am happy you are reading this book. This means you did not give up even when you wanted to. You stayed, fought, or had prayer warriors praying on your behalf.

I will never forget my grandfather, Pastor Ronald Leonard. He was a prayer warrior. He hit the streets of York, Pennsylvania, with other pastors and his church community to pray. He stayed faithful and went from street to street and corner to corner. Loving yourself has many layers. Knowing who you are is a good start:

- learning your likes and dislikes
- learning what triggers you and what grows you
- what moves you forward and what sets you back
- knowing what you're goals are and your purpose in life

Make yourself a priority with self-care. Take some alone time with trips away from parenthood, careers, and decision-making. It took me years to figure out what self-care was. It meant disconnecting, putting myself first and learning music. Sometimes, I would go to the beach and listen to the waves. I listened to encouraging people and their stories, like Sarah Jakes Roberts, Jamal and Natasha Miller, Dr. Faith Wokoma, Dr. Anita Phillips, T.D. Jakes and my pastors Apostle Sam Wagner and Dr. Rico Wagner. Their guidance of the Bible and helped me through the world's battles. They helped me stick to the word of God. I always felt empowered and closer to my calling and fell more deeply in love with the person I was, who I was becoming and loving myself. I used to think that spending time with my children and doing whatever they needed was self-love. That was loving them. One year, I learned I could do both. Then, I learned that without loving myself, there was no love to give to anyone else. I had to choose myself first and become the best version of me before giving it to anyone else.

Self- Reflection Questions:

1. What does self-love mean to you?

____

____

____

____

____

____

2. What do you do for you and to love you?

3. What obstacles do you face when this happens? How do you overcome the obstacles that interfere with loving you?

4. Name a few things you enjoy when it comes to loving you.

This is all foreign to you and you are saying love on me how do you do that. Start making yourself a priority, start to block out your time on your calendar. Identify what hurts you and hold you back from loving you.

Always remember you are fearfully and wonderfully made there is nothing you cannot do or overcome.

CHAPTER 30

Loving You Prayer:

Lord, give us the strength to love ourselves like you love us. The Lord gives us the eyes to see the greatness in us. Give us the strength to choose every day. Confirm that taking care of us is not selfish but necessary. Keep making things clear and kick down every stronghold, barrier, detour, and roadblock blocking us from loving ourselves. Show us how you see us and not the world. In Jesus' name, Amen.

CHAPTER 31

Spiritual Journey

Who is God? Is there more than one God in the world? The answer is yes, but what do you believe? My grandparents taught me the right way to live. I went to Sunday school and children's church; we served God. We learned the truth of His Word from the Bible. In 2025, so much has changed regarding the expectation of pastors' position and teaching the Word of God. Many now lead and rely on their own thoughts and feelings.

Self- Reflection Questions:

1. What does the Word of God mean to you?

____

____

____

____

____

____

2. Do you have a church home?

3. Do you have spiritual people in your life?

4. Do you believe that prayers change things?

5. At one point, did you go to church and stop? What was the reason?

____

____

____

____

____

____

6. Do you feel like you are called to serve in the church to help change the lives of others? What is holding you back?

____

____

____

____

____

____

CHAPTER 32

Spiritual Journey Prayer

Lord, I pray that you have your way with the person reading this book. I pray that they identify the life you have for them and find ways to draw closer to you and experience your everlasting love and healing for their lives. I pray that you send people who know your word to help support, uplift, and carry them into this next season. I pray that they hear you and experience you right where they are in this very moment and that they know you are not the author of confusion. In Jesus' name, Amen.

CHAPTER 33

Identify Trauma Or Unfortunate Events

We all have memories or moments we would like to forget and wish never happened to us. When we look back or relive them, we ask God the following:

- Why me?
- Why did you let this happen to me?
- Why didn't you protect me?
- Why am I suffering so much?
- Why don't others suffer?
- Why can't I be a happy person?
- Why do I have so much pain?
- Why am I not healed?
- How do I heal?
- I will never forget what they did to me. The moments or memories in my head will not leave. I keep reliving those dark moments and secrets no one knows anything about.
- Did I deserve what happened to me?
- Will I always be unhappy?
- Where is my joy?

- This cannot be the life you have designed for me to live. Why do I lack?
- After everything I have been through, why me Lord?
- Please help me! The pain that I feel is killing me slowly and I need help. I need change and a way out.

Have you asked yourself any of the above questions? Was this from an event that caused trauma in your life? What is trauma? It is a deep disturbing experience. Forms of trauma can be acute, chronic, or complex. Most trauma stems from childhood abandonment, sex, physical and verbal abuse, domestic violence and death.

Self- Reflection Questions:

1. Can you think of an event in your life that has left you with some sort of trauma? Do you feel trapped?

____

____

____

____

____

____

2. List any events in your life that you may feel left a negative impact on your life. Is this holding you back from living life?

____

____

____

3. What happened?

4. Who was involved?

5. What has caused you pain?

6. What are your triggers? What makes you emotional or uncomfortable?

7. Where is the pain when you are triggered? Who does it remind you of? What event does it remind you of? Who caused the pain?

8. Do you carry this pain wherever you go?

9. Does this affect your daily life in relationships, decision-making, and moving forward?

CHAPTER 34

Identify Trauma Or Unfortunate Events Prayer

Lord, only you know about the things we do not speak. I ask that you set us free from any unhealed trauma that has entered our lives. I ask that you help us remember who, what and when so that we can heal and begin to release those unfortunate events that took place in our lives. I ask that you teach us how to forgive. I ask that you release any shame or confusion this may have caused. I pray that we know and receive that there is a fulfilled life after trauma. We will survive and overcome, even if we are broken in this very moment. We know that you can restore us. Help us navigate this journey, knowing that you will never leave or forsake us and that your love never fails. By your stripes, we are healed. Healing is our portion. In Jesus' name. Amen.

CHAPTER 35

Surround Yourself With A Network Of Support.

There are times in life when you feel alone more times than others. It may seem as if you do not have any genuine loving support. You may be in a season of not trusting anyone because of past experiences or moments. What is support? I grew up having trust issues. When I had children, because of my abuse, I never trusted anyone. Growing up without trusting anyone will ruin your life. You always fear what is going to happen next. I am pretty sure that my children missed out on some things because of my fear and lack of trust in others. I had a fear of them being abused.

One day, my daughter's therapist told me I must trust and be at peace. I raised my children, and they listened to me. I trusted them to take what I showed them and apply it. At that moment, I realized I had been in some way holding them back from bonding time with friends and family because of my fear. At the moment, it felt like the best decision, but I realized my unhealed experience led me to believe in the worst scenarios. Whenever my children wanted to try something different and leave the house to have new friends, I feared the worst. This prepared them for real life, but it was unhealthy at times. From this day forward, I try to look at things differently and allow them to be children and not live in fear.

I was not used to people doing things for me. I was always the one helping others and giving to them. At times, I felt people did not show up for me like I showed up for them. I did not do things to receive something back. My mind and heart are not wired that way. As I went through different seasons, I felt like I always gave more than I received. I never trusted anyone, but one day, I wanted to trust. I will never forget the day I started to trust again. I was part of a program called Bridge of Hope. In the program, I had a team of volunteers called my neighboring volunteers. They heard my needs and gathered to support me. It was so simple. I wanted patio furniture; it was such a simple request I mentioned to my neighbor volunteers and one day, I came home to a patio furniture set up on my back porch. I was in awe and thought, "Wait! There are people in the world who will do for you without wanting anything in return?"

Self- Reflection Questions:

1. Can you think of three people who showed up for you in a time of need?

____

____

____

____

____

____

2. Do you show up for them?

3. How have they helped you?

4. How have you helped them?

5. If you cannot think of anyone, is this because you will not allow anyone to help you?

6. Do you have an issue with trusting others?

7. How can you begin to trust again? Do you want to trust others?

8. What stops you from connecting with and trusting others?

CHAPTER 36

Seeking Professional Assistance

Every culture is different. We all have different backgrounds, but the stigma grows if you see a therapist. Something is wrong with you or you're an outcast. Sometimes we need an unbiased opinion to hear us out, to listen to our internal battles to identify things we did not know about ourselves that may hinder or be harmful to us such as our choices, patterns, lifestyles, children, finances, and relationships. God and therapy saved my life at my lowest point in life. There are therapists for traumatic relationships and childhood professionals, who specialize in helping people who are overloaded with daily life. Therapy has uncovered areas of concern that I did not even know I had. It also brought out the best version of me. We do not know what we do not know. Once we do, we can take our time and work on it. Therapy is a game changer; it is important to have your children start therapy at a young age. Life has given us experiences we did not ask for and grief that never ends, but with God and therapy, we will live again. We will find ourselves again. We will find our true identities and purpose. We will become whole and happiness will live within us.

Self- Reflection Questions:

1. What are some areas of life that you do not like to talk about?

____

____

____

____

____

____

2. Do you find yourself sad at times for unknown reasons?

____

____

____

____

____

____

3. Are you easily triggered?

____

____

____

____

4. Do you have a hard time letting go? Do you feel stuck?

Depending on the answers to the above questions, you may want to seek professional guidance to help you get started on your process. In addition, reach out to local churches for support groups and prayer calls.

CHAPTER 37

Seeking Professional Assistance Prayer

Lord, I pray that shame or the voices of others do not hold us back from seeking professional help or connecting with local churches or prayer lines. I pray that you speak to us individually and uncover what we need. I pray that help is on the way and that everyone that we need on our journey will come our way with confirmation from you directly. Order our steps Lord for the plans that you have for our lives. Let us realize that our plan may not look like others we know but we trust your plan for our healing in Jesus' name, amen.

CHAPTER 38

Release The Trauma. Working On Your Identity

For years, I was hidden behind the identity of being a mother, going to school, a sister, a friend, a cousin, a girlfriend, a people pleaser, and everything but what I really was. One day, someone asked me who I was, and she said I could not use my kids and job to define who I was. I thought, "Wow, who am I? Who is Berlesha Palmer without kids, work, and school?" I was stuck and could not answer. After that question, I began to work on myself to understand who I was. What do I like? I always please others, so I was truly unsure who I was. After that day, I was determined to learn who I was. I needed to understand who I was and introduce myself by my identity and not the identity that people gave me. My life experiences or life story were never really me. Let us take some time to examine our thoughts and hearts.

Self- Reflection Questions:

1. What did others tell you about yourself growing up?

____

____

2. Who do others say your identity is?

3. What do you say your identity is?

4. Who are you?

5. What experiences affected your views on who you are?

6. What things are you holding on to keep you somewhere you do not belong?

CHAPTER 39

Release The Trauma. Working On Your Identity Prayer

Lord, I pray that the person reading this book will hear from you about the identity that you have given them and all the great things that come with their God given identities and purpose for their lives. I pray for the release of all the word curses over their lives that didn't come from you. I pray this is the first step in becoming who you created them to be in Jesus' name. Amen.

CHAPTER 40

Show Up And Show Out For You First

Now that we have unpacked so much, it is time for us to show up. How does one show up for self? You are putting yourself first by doing self-care or leaving something for yourself. You cannot pour from an empty cup, heart, or soul. Put yourself first. For those who are used to being last, they do not always know how to put themselves first. I started by changing my surroundings. I prayed and I sought professional help through therapy to reveal what was holding me back. Speak life into yourself. Stay surrounded by people who want to see you be the best version of yourself. Even when people can show up for you, choose to show up for yourself. Look in the mirror and be transparent about what you love about yourself and what you need to work on, then form a plan to get there. Speak words of affirmation over your life. Find out your identity through Christ first and man second.

Do not let people label you as someone you are not. Start to do things you enjoy that bring happiness to your heart and soul. Do not attach your happiness, identity, past, or present to people. Be true to yourself and your identity. Do not let others define you and set you back or hold you hostage. Stand bold in who you are and who God called you to be. Learn His words, find a church home, join some supporting groups, and surround yourself with people where you are trying to go, and those who can mentor and fill you with knowledge. Choose yourself today and every day moving forward. No one comes before you. Starting today, you will always choose yourself first and never doubt yourself. Never speak down on yourself. The sky is the limit and you can have whatever you want.

CHAPTER 41

Make Peace With Your Past And Give It To God.

At times, we can stay stuck in the past. Life is moving on and we just feel stuck. We are physically moving, but internally, we are stuck in the past. We have good memories from the past and some that are not so great. Yet somehow, as we continue to live, we always find ourselves in the past: relationships, friendships, states, cities, suffering, hurt, and pain. If we let it, all the things from the past somehow become a part of who we are. Sometimes, it is the truth, and other times, it is a lie, depending on how we view things. The past will make or break your life. It will enhance or destroy your life. It will set you free or hold you in bondage. Our past experiences can block or withhold our blessings. It can keep us lacking or in disagreement with what God has said we should have. If you do not make peace with your past, it can torment all aspects of your future. To make peace with our past, what should we do? Where do we start? I am glad you asked.

Self- Reflection Questions:

1. Who do you need to forgive from the past?

____

____

____

____

____

____

2. What did they do?

____

____

____

____

____

____

3. Why haven't you forgiven them?

____

____

____

____

4. What have you buried in the past that you do not want to face?

5. Take a moment and write it out.

6. What events from your past stick out?

7. What events from your past play in your present time and future?

8. What in your past is holding you back? Old relationships? Being angry? Forgiveness? Pain and sorrow?

CHAPTER 42

New Beginnings

New beginnings were hard for me, so at times I stayed stuck in the past. Whether it was someone I loved, a decision I made, or something I could have done differently, past hurts or disappointment. I realized staying in the past and referring to the past held me hostage and year after year, I was going by whether I was stuck on someone who hurt me or what we could have been. I should not have been waiting for them to rise to the occasion, but the truth is, people are who they are and will always show you what they are comfortable with. More importantly, they will do what you allow. How did you teach people how to treat you? How can we teach anyone to treat us a certain way when we do not know how to treat, love, or care for ourselves?

Turn your hurt and pain into your testimony to help and save others. You will eventually heal. It will take time and be uncomfortable, but there is nothing in this world more important than the healed version of yourself. There is nothing more important than your story and identity. You will overcome all the things sent to take you out, to hold you back, to give you a false identity, to steal your joy, to block and delay your blessings, and to keep you in unhealed relationships and places in life. You deserve to prosper, grow, and fulfill all your dreams with love and support. The pain serves a purpose even though we can feel like, "God, you could have skipped that part or that process."

All the pain serves a purpose. This is why you are strong and overcome the things that were meant to destroy you. You made it to share your story and testimony with someone else. You went through it to help someone else, to prevent someone else from experiencing the same things, and to break generational curses. Don't hide, protect, or condone those who need love and healing to change the narrative for you, your children, and your children's children. Stand as who you are, whether it is good or painful. Your story is yours, whether happy or sad. No one can tell your story like you. Do not rush or skip the process. Trust the process but remember to work through it. People need you, your voice, your words, and your story.

Self- Reflection Questions:

1. What is your story?

____

____

____

____

____

____

2. Are you ready to share your story with others?

____

____

____

____

3. Do you share your story now? How and when do you share your story?

4. Think about a time you shared your story. What happened? Did you encourage someone? Did you save someone?

CHAPTER 43

The Power Of Your Story

You never know the power of your story until you find the courage to share it with others and because you made it through to share your story, this is now your testimony. You have passed the test and made it, which means you are set free from the test. There is an old saying, "A closed mouth will not get fed." Open your mouth. Share your story and feed the people. This is to encourage you. There is someone right now trying to figure out how to endure the storm and test that you already have the answers to. You and your story are an answered prayer. Do not be ashamed of your journey. The test and tribulations have made you into who you are today. Stand in victory. You are not where you used to be and count all the wins throughout the process until you get to where you need to be. At times, we forget the losses. If it were not for the losses, we could never win. They shape, mold, and prepare us to do better and to overcome victory. If we lose again that's okay because we now know how to overcome the loss.

CHAPTER 44

What's Next: What Tools Do You Need To Be Successful?

What does success mean to you? What is next for my life? I have learned the world has a definition of what success should look like. Over the last few years, I have learned that success means something different to every person in the world. Success for me is learning God's word and His identity for my life. It is seating God first in my heart and everything after Him. I am learning that success is to witness beautiful moments and capture them with my family. Success is to love myself and those around me. Success is serving in my church and having a humble heart. Success is rooting for people's accomplishments and happiness. Success is supporting, encouraging, and uplifting others. It's about helping people to heal and setting their souls free. Success is knowing my worth and not settling for anything less than what I am supposed to have. Success is limitless. There is no right or wrong definition of success.

Self- Reflection Questions:

1. What does success mean to you?

2. What makes you successful?

3. Do you have work to do to be successful?

4. What are your six-month goals?

5. What are your three-year goals?

6. What are your five-year goals?

7. Who is your support system? Do you need a support system?

8. How long will it take you to get where you want to be?

9. What are the action steps that need to happen next to get there?

WHAT'S NEXT: WHAT TOOLS DO YOU NEED TO BE SUCCESSFUL?

CHAPTER 45

What's Next: What Tools Do You Need To Be Successful?

Prayer:

Thank you Lord. We know that your will is already done. You said you know the plans that you have for our lives. We trust you and pray that we will align with your plans for our lives. I pray that every person reading this book can view themselves in a different light, your light. I pray for the peace that surpasses all understanding. Meet and touch every person where they are today. I pray after this day, you take them higher and higher, and they surrender and follow your steps into the destination you called them in this season. In Jesus' Name, Amen.

CHAPTER 46

Scriptures

Psalms 139:14 *I am fearfully and wonderful made.*

Psalms 147:3 *God heals the broken hearted.*

Psalms 46:10 *Be still and know that I am God.*

Jeremiah 29:11 *For I know the plans I have for you said the lord plans to prosper you.*

1 Corinthians 13:4 *Love is patient, love is kind, It does not envy, it does not boast, it is not proud, it's not rude, it does not seek its own interests, it not irritable, it does not keep a record of wrongs, it does not keep a record of wrongs, it does not rejoice at wrong doing.*

2 Corinthians 5:7 *We Walk by faith and not by but sight.*

Ephesians 3:20 *Now to him who is able to do exceedingly abundantly above all that we ask or think according to the power that works in us.*

Healing:

Psalms 147:3 *"He heals the brokenhearted and binds up their wounds."*

Psalm 30:2 *"Lord my God, I called to You for help, and you healed me."*

Jeremiah 17:14 *"Heal me, Lord, and I will be healed: save me and I will be saved, for you are the one I praise.*

Self-Identity:

1 Corinthians 13:13 *Love is the greatest of the three remaining things: faith, hope., love.*

Genesis 1:27 *We are made in God's image, and our core identity is shaped by God.*

In Conclusion

I encourage you to keep the faith too. Your testimony is your tool to healing. No one can tell your story the way that you can. No matter how bad you think it is, someone needs to hear your story in order to survive. Allow God to lead and the rest will follow. It doesn't matter where you start, just remember faith over fear. Stay encouraged and never give up. It only gets better in time. I pray that this book blesses you and someone you know. I pray for restoration and healing in your life. I pray for God to show up in your life in only the ways He can and if you don't have a relationship with the Lord, I pray that this book will lead you to a Bible base church to teach and help you grow into the person the Lord has called you to be.

Thank you, Lord, to every person who reads this book. Thank you for the things that need to be revealed through the words that you have given me. Thank you for allowing me to be transparent and obedient to your directions. I hope people are set free from their past and the bondages holding them back. I thank you for clarity. We ask that you remove any confusion, uncertainty, or setbacks, any relationship that may be holding them back from their God given identity, which was given to them before birth while placed in their mother's womb. I pray that all those may find their purpose or refine their purpose through healing and showing up as their best selves in who you created them to be. I pray that forgiveness has begun to take place, and the right healthy relationships are being developed as we speak. We are free and will rest in your arms. You are a prayer away and your love protects us. In Jesus' name. Amen.

Until next time......
Xo,
Lesha

About The Author

Berlesha Palmer is a woman of God, a mom, and a powerful intercessor. Berlesha (Lesha) Palmer is from a small town in York, PA. She relocated to Tampa, Florida, and then eventually to North Carolina. She is a proud mother of a son, who graduated high school a year early and became a CDL truck driver at 18, traveling across the world. She has a daughter who recently graduated high school early and is starting her college career soon. Berlesha (Lesha) Palmer is a graduate of William Penn Senior High School. She spent most of her high school years at Central High School and ended her senior year at William Penn Senior High School (York High). She graduated from the Consolidated School of Business with a degree in legal administration, and she is currently enrolled in her senior year of college at Purdue Global University, majoring in legal studies. She is a human resource professional by day in the finance, fin-tech, and higher education industry, specializing in employee relations, training, and development. She is a Bridge of Hope York Program graduate and a proud graduate of the Martin Luther King Leadership Program. She is a faithful member of New Foundation Church International, where she serves on the New Element Youth ministry and greeting/guest services ministry. She enjoys traveling and eating authentic food, seafood, rice, and pasta in her free time. She enjoys reading spiritual and encouraging books in her free time. The beach is one of her favorite places to visit.

"Trauma Is My Testimony," is a book is a powerful resource for the Listening Ear Organization. A listening ear is an organization that God laid on Berlesha Palmer's heart. We all need an ear and a shoulder to lean on for support and guidance when we feel like no one is there. No matter the issues we face, a listening ear is always here to help 24 hours a day to be a layer of support as we navigate through the changes of life. For more information, please contact alisteningear2024@gmail.com to start your healing process or to navigate through the layers of healing. To donate, become a donor, partner with the movement, be a prayer warrior, mentor, or serve at a work related or school functions, please contact: alisteningear2024@gmail.com.

A Listening Ear mission statement: To help others find their true identities by overcoming the most traumatic experiences. To heal, encourage and supply life tools to navigate through hurt, pain, and disappointment. Growing closer to God to help heal souls in the way that only He can do. Your life is not over. It is just the beginning. Trust the process of healing. Trust the process of your network and most importantly, trust God's timing.

www.ingramcontent.com/pod-product-compliance
Lightning Source LLC
LaVergne TN
LVHW022058200926
848481LV00003B/973